HAWAII

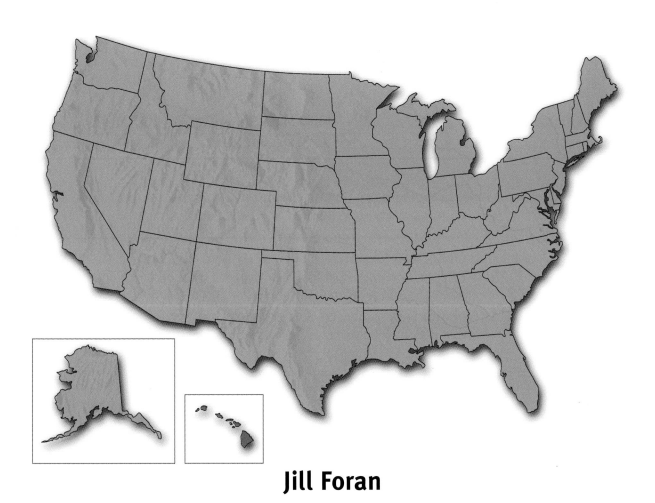

Jill Foran

Published by Weigl Publishers Inc.
123 South Broad Street, Box 227
Mankato, MN   56002
USA

Library of Congress Cataloging-in-Publication Data available upon
request from the publisher. Fax: (507) 388-2746 for the attention of the
Publishing Records Department.

ISBN 1-930954-50-6

Printed in the United States of America
1 2 3 4 5 6 7 8 9 0   05 04 03 02 01

Editor
Rennay Craats
Design
Warren Clark
Cover Design
Terry Paulhus
Copy Editor
Heather Kissock
Layout
Derek Heck

Photograph Credits
Every reasonable effort has been made to trace ownership and to obtain
permission to reprint copyright material. The publishers would be
pleased to have any errors or omissions brought to their attention so
that they may be corrected in subsequent printings.

Cover: Young hula girl (Jack Hollingsworth, Hawai'i Convention and Visitors Bureau),
Lei (Jeff Greenburg, Visuals Unlimited); **Archive Photos:** pages 16B-L, 18M-L, 18B-L,
25T-L (Reuters/Rose Prouser), 28B-L (Popperfoto); **Bishop Museum, Hawaii:** pages
3M-L, 15T-L, 16B-L, 17T-L, 17B-L, 19M-L, 21M-R, 22B-L; **Corel Corporation:** pages
3T-L, 4T-L, 4M, 4B-L, 4B-R, 5T-L, 5T-L, 6B, 7B-L, 8B-L, 9M-L, 9B-L, 9T-R, 9B-R, 10T-
L, 10B-L, 11T-L, 11B-R, 11B-L, 12T-L, 12B-R, 12B-L, 13T-L, 14B-R, 16T-L, 21B-L,
22T-L, 22B-R, 23M-L, 23B-R, 24T-L, 24B-L, 27M-L, 27B-L, 27B-R, 28B-R; **Eyewire
Corporation:** page 28T-R; **Hawaii's Visitors and Convention Bureau:** pages 3T-R, 3B-
L, 3B-R, 5T-R, 6T-L, 6M-R (Phil Spalding), 7M-R (William Waterfall), 7B, 8T-L (Peter
French), 10B-R (Maui Ocean Center),12T-L (Joe Solem), 13B-R, 14T-L (Robert
Coello), 14B-L, 15T-R, 15B-M (Douglas Peebles), 17B-R, 18T-L, 19T-R, 19B, 20T-L
(Jack Hollingsworth), 20B-L (Douglas Peebles), 20B-R, 21T-L, 23T-R, 25B-L, 27T-L
(Robert Holmes) 28T-L, 29T-L; **Map Town Ltd.:** 8B; **Photo Disc Corporation:** 26T-
L,26T-R, 26B-R, 26B-L; **Visuals Unlimited:** 5B-L.

CONTENTS

INTRODUCTION

Hawaii is called the Aloha State. Aloha is a Hawaiian word with many meanings: welcome, love, hello, and goodbye. The word aloha reveals the warm and welcoming nature of the Hawaiian people. Visitors from around the world come to Hawaii to enjoy its tropical paradise.

QUICK FACTS

Hawaii was the last state to enter the Union.

Honolulu is the capital of Hawaii. It is on the island of Oahu.

The state bird is the Nene, or Hawaiian Goose. The Nene nearly became extinct, but was rescued by conservationists throughout the world.

Hawaii's state flower is the yellow hibiscus.

The state tree is the kukui tree. It is also known as the candlenut.

Hawaii's state song is "Hawaii Ponoi– Hawaii's Own."

Many hotels and resorts line Hawaii's beaches.

Getting There

Hawaii is the most isolated population center in the world. It is 2,390 miles from California, 3,850 miles from Japan, 4,900 miles from China, and 5,280 miles from the Philippines. These distances do not stop millions of visitors from coming to the Aloha State every year. Driving to the islands from the mainland is not possible, but many airlines offer regular flights to Hawaii. Hawaii has thirty airports to accommodate the large number of flights. You can also take a boat to Hawaii. Cruise ships and other boats frequent the waters surrounding Hawaii.

Aloha Airlines provides more than 170 flights to the neighboring islands every day.

Location Map

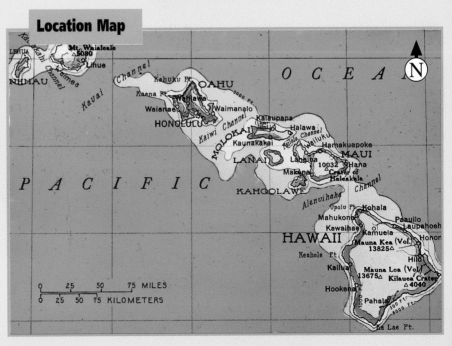

Hawaii is made up of eight main islands: Hawaii, Maui, Molokai, Lanai, Oahu, Kauai, Nihau, and Kahoolawe. Hawaii also includes 124 **islets**.

The island of Hawaii is nicknamed the Big Island because it is by far the largest island. It is best known for its volcanoes. Much of the island is covered in volcanic ash and lava beds.

Maui is nicknamed the Valley Isle because its two volcanic mountains are separated by **lush** land. Maui's rich red soil lines the roads and provides great land for growing and farming.

The Friendly Isle, Molokai, is known for its friendly people. Each region on the island is very different. One region has mountains and high cliffs, and another has dry land used mainly for cattle ranching. The last region is covered with pineapple plantations.

QUICK FACTS

Hawaii's islands are almost all volcanic in origin.

Each of Hawaii's inhabited islands has a nickname.

Maui is the second largest island in Hawaii.

Many of Hawaii's waterfalls and pools were formed by ancient lava beds.

Lanai is called the Private Island because few tourists know they can visit it. Oahu, called the Gathering Place, is the most populated island. Pearl Harbor is on Oahu's southern coast. Honolulu, the state's capital, is also on Oahu.

Kauai is nicknamed the Garden Isle because of its lush greens and its many streams and waterfalls. Kauai receives more rain than any of the other islands. The rain has worn away much of the land and carved out Kauai's steep canyons and cliffs.

Nihau is called the Forbidden Island because the public cannot visit it. Nihau is private property. A woman named Elizabeth Sinclair bought the island in 1864. Her descendants now live there and operate a cattle ranch that covers almost the entire island.

Honolulu, on the island of Oahu, is a lively city with many museums and art galleries.

QUICK FACTS

Lanai was once owned by the Dole Food Company. It used to be known as Pineapple Island.

The island of Hawaii is almost twice the size of all the other islands combined.

Kahoolawe does not have a nickname. No one lives there. It is the smallest of the islands, and its land cannot grow much. For a while, the United States Army, Navy, and Air Force used Kahoolawe for target practice.

LAND AND CLIMATE

When you stand on one of the Hawaiian Islands, you are actually standing on piles of lava. Hawaii is made of volcanoes built up from the ocean floor. The chain of islands has been forming for years. On the ocean floor, there is a hot spot where volcanic activity causes lava to flow out of a vent. For millions of years, the lava added layer upon layer to itself. Massive volcanoes were finally forced above the surface of the ocean.

Once above sea level, the islands were shaped by the sea, rain, and wind. Nature has given each island its unique appearance. They have steep cliffs, deep caves, wide valleys, lush rain forests, miles of coastal plains, and huge volcanic mountains.

Hawaii's climate is almost always pleasant. Winter temperatures barely differ from summer temperatures. They range between 72° F and 79° F throughout the year. **Trade winds** keep the Hawaiian climate agreeable all year.

QUICK FACTS

The highest temperature recorded in Hawaii was 100° F on April 27, 1931. The lowest temperature ever recorded in Hawaii was on May 17, 1979. It was 12° F.

Waialeale Mountain on the island of Kauai is one of the wettest spots in the world. It receives about 460 inches of rainfall per year.

The Big Island of Hawaii is home to two active volcanoes: Mauna Loa and Kilauea.

Mauna Loa is the most massive mountain on Earth. It occupies an area of 19,000 cubic miles.

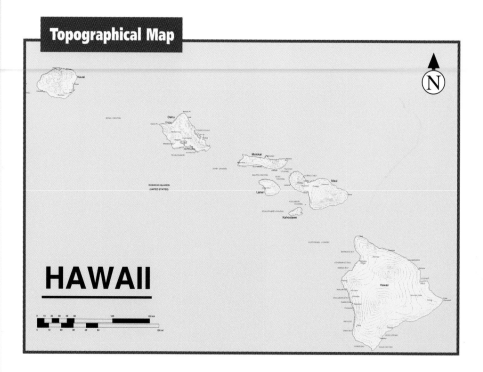

Topographical Map

HAWAII

NATURAL RESOURCES

Imagine having a shortage of water when you are surrounded by the Pacific Ocean! Hawaiians have access to all the salt water they want, but when it comes to fresh water, their supply is limited. There are a number of streams, ponds, and waterfalls on the islands, but there are no big lakes to supply fresh water. Hawaiians depend on rainfall for much of their fresh water. Rain seeps through the rocky surface of the land and creates large underground reserves of fresh water. Thick growths of tropical plants and trees grow in areas where the rainfall is heaviest.

Hawaii's soil is good for growing tropical fruits and plants. Sugarcane and pineapple are the most important crops on the islands. They are key contributors to Hawaii's economy. The land is also good for growing macadamia nuts, coffee, and fruit, including guavas, mangoes, and papayas.

Hawaiian pineapples have long been considered the most flavorful pineapples in the world.

QUICK FACTS

About 10 percent of Hawaii's soil is very fertile. There are huge areas of **barren** lava rock where soil is weak or non-existent.

Hawaii has no important mineral or oil deposits. Most mining is limited to recovering crushed stone and cement. Mining stone and cement are important for building roads.

Hawaii generates its electricity by using oil as fuel, but there are no oil deposits on any of the islands. Hawaiians import oil from other countries for their electrical energy.

PLANTS AND ANIMALS

There are very few land animals in Hawaii that are native to the islands. Only land snails, insects, a rare bat species, and a number of birds can claim native status. Human settlers brought all of Hawaii's other animals to the islands. These included dogs, cats, horses, cows, goats, pigs, reptiles, and amphibians.

Life in the ocean is much more diverse than on land. More than 600 species of fish swim in Hawaiian waters. About one-third of these fish can be found only in Hawaii. The fish share their waters with dolphins, sharks, humpback whales, and sea turtles.

QUICK FACTS

Wild animals in Hawaii are usually domesticated stock gone astray. Wild pigs and goats have done a lot of damage to vegetation and soil.

Hawaii's unofficial state fish is the humuhumunukunuku apua'a. It is also known as the Rectangular Triggerfish.

There are 5,000 varieties of the hibiscus flower in Hawaii.

The Pacific sea turtle, found in Hawaii, has longer limbs than the Atlantic sea turtle.

Many plants grew in Hawaii long before human settlers arrived. Seeds carried by birds, wind, and ocean tides likely caused the early plant life to flourish. Settlers later introduced new plants to Hawaii. Polynesian settlers brought edible plants such as coconut, **taro**, banana, and sugarcane. They also brought the kukui tree, which is the state tree. Later, settlers introduced many exotic flowers.

Hawaii's environment is very delicate. The main islands are slowly being worn down. Nature's elements are gradually **eroding** the volcanic mountains. People contribute to the damage by overusing the land. Hawaiians are aware of their fragile surroundings and are now taking measures to protect their land.

State and national parks help prevent further erosion caused by humans. Hawaii has more than seventy state parks and two important national parks: Haleakala National Park on Maui, and Volcanoes National Park on the Big Island of Hawaii. These parks preserve natural settings and protect plants and animals.

Wind can destroy banana plants. Light winds shred the leaves and stronger winds can twist the whole plant, causing root damage.

QUICK FACTS

The kukui, or candlenut tree, was very useful to early Hawaiians. The kukui nut provided oil for lamps and medicine for sealing cuts. While fishing, Hawaiians would spit chewed kukui kernels into the ocean to calm the waters.

Plants and flowers are in bloom all year on the islands.

TOURISM

The beauty and attractions of the Hawaiian Islands draw millions of visitors each year. At Diamond Head or Punchbowl, both in Honolulu, tourists can see the remnants of an extinct volcanic vent. The Arizona Memorial, also in Honolulu, is a tribute to American soldiers in World War II. Other interesting sites for tourists are the royal Iolani Palace and the Polynesian Cultural Center. At the cultural center, visitors can walk around replicas of Polynesian villages.

The beaches are probably the main attraction for many visitors. The islands have miles of white sand beaches. Honolulu's Waikiki Beach is one of the most famous beaches in the world. It offers just about any watersport, beach front shops, and plenty of sunshine. Other beaches in the state are equally appealing. The beautiful black sand beaches on the Big Island are also popular tourist spots.

Diamond Head was named by early explorers who thought the glittering face of this Hawaiian mountain actually contained diamonds.

QUICK FACTS

Hawaii is home to many luxury hotels and resorts. The Hyatt Regency Waikola cost $360 million to build. It is one of the most expensively constructed hotels in the world.

Honolulu alone has more than 50 miles of beaches.

Iolani Palace is the only royal palace in the United States.

The sand on the Big Island is black due to its contact with hot lava from volcanic eruptions.

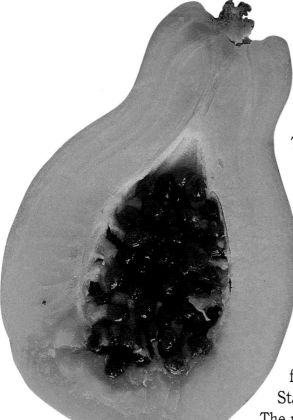

INDUSTRY

Tourism is Hawaii's most successful industry. Almost 7 million tourists visit the state each year.

Another leading source of income in Hawaii is food processing. Sugarcane is processed into raw sugar or molasses and is then sent to the mainland. Similarly, pineapple is canned, frozen, or juiced and then sold on the mainland. Tropical fruit, such as guava and papaya, are often processed into jams and jellies.

Hawaii's location in the Pacific Ocean is ideal for military defense. There are major United States marine, army, and air force bases in Hawaii. The presence of the military plays a vital role in Hawaii's economy. Military spending on construction and maintenance provides local Hawaiians with jobs and business opportunities.

QUICK FACTS

The first successful flight between the mainland and Hawaii was in 1927. Two Army lieutenants flew from Oakland to Oahu in 25 hours and 50 minutes. Air travel opened up a world of opportunity for Hawaii's tourism industry.

Military personnel and their families account for 100,000 of the people living in Hawaii.

The first successful sugarcane plantation in Hawaii was in 1835. Soon after, pioneers began moving to Hawaii to grow sugarcane.

GOODS AND SERVICES

Hawaii is very isolated from the rest of the United States, so it is completely dependent on sea and air transportation for its economic growth. Ships carry and deliver most of the food, consumer goods, and raw materials used in Hawaii. **Imported** consumer products add to the high cost of living on the islands. Everything is more expensive because it is harder to get.

Despite the reliance on imports, Hawaii does export some products. The state's leading exports are raw sugar, molasses, pineapples, clothing, flowers, and cement.

In Britain's early days, pineapples were considered so precious that King Charles II posed with one to show his power.

QUICK FACTS

There are six daily newspapers, six television stations, and more than forty radio stations in the state.

Before World War II, a few short railroads were built on some of the islands. They were used for transferring sugar, pineapples, and military supplies. Today, only one of these railroads still runs. It is on Maui and operates as a tourist line.

The islands are not only isolated from the mainland, they are also isolated from one another. Transportation is difficult because the islands are so far apart. Maui to Kauai is more than swimming distance apart. Airplanes fly between the islands so that visitors and Hawaiians alike can get to other parts of the state. Hawaii has thirty airports to accommodate the air traffic.

The Mt. Kilaueu volcano is best seen from a small airplane or helicopter.

The North Shore of Kauai was once the site of a famous hula school. Chanters would stand at the edge of the sea and test their voices against the crashing of the waves.

FIRST NATIONS

The first people to set foot on the Hawaiian Islands were Polynesian voyagers. Sometime around the seventh century, these voyagers left their homes on other Pacific Islands and sailed to Hawaii. These people named the area "Hawaii."

There are two theories about the naming of the islands. Many people believe that the Polynesian chief Hawaii Loa discovered the islands. The settlers may have named Hawaii after him. However, it is also possible that the islands were named after Hawaiki, which is the name of the traditional Polynesian homeland.

After the initial discovery of the Hawaiian Islands, waves of Polynesian immigrants, mostly from the island of Tahiti, came to Hawaii. The islands became divided into several kingdoms, each ruled by a separate chief. The kingdoms were often at war with one another. There was no unity among the land.

When Polynesian settlers came to Hawaii, they cleared the land to grow taro, sweet potato, banana, and other plants.

EXPLORERS AND MISSIONARIES

The Hawaiian Islands remained unknown to the rest of the world until the late eighteenth century. Captain James Cook of Great Britain discovered the islands in 1778. Soon after Cook's discovery, traders and explorers began to arrive. Hawaii became an important **port** for European and North American ships that were on their way to trade their goods in East Asia. Foreign ships would remain in Hawaiian harbors for months.

Local chiefs still ruled the islands at the time of Cook's discovery. In 1782, a chief named Kamehameha began a ten-year war in an attempt to gain control of all the islands. By 1810, Kamehameha had captured and unified the Hawaiian Islands. His success was due largely to the firearms he obtained from traders and explorers who stopped at his port. Kamehameha became King Kamehameha I, the first ruler of unified Hawaii.

QUICK FACTS

British explorer James Cook named the Hawaiian Islands the Sandwich Islands, in honor of his **patron**, the Earl of Sandwich. The name did not stick.

The first group of missionaries arrived in Hawaii in 1820. The group was led by Hiram Bingham, a minister from New England.

Missionaries set up schools, and helped to develop the Hawaiian alphabet.

The Captain James Cook Monument honors the famous British explorer. Hawaiians believed he symbolized the Hawaiian god, Lono.

EARLY SETTLERS

King Kamehameha was very careful about keeping Hawaiian independence. In his contact with foreign visitors, Kamehameha adopted items that he felt would help his people lead better lives and banned items he believed would harm them.

Foreigners introduced cattle, horses, and plants to the native Hawaiians. They also introduced a number of infectious diseases. The Hawaiian people had lived in isolation for many years and did not have the **immunities** to fight these diseases. Many of them died.

King Kamehameha I died in 1819. His son became his successor, and took the name Kamehameha II. One of the king's first acts was to get rid of the local Hawaiian religion. This religion included the belief in many gods and goddesses, and human sacrifice.

QUICK FACTS

Hawaii's population was estimated at 300,000 before explorers and traders arrived in the late 1700s. By 1820, the population of native inhabitants had fallen to 135,000.

Hawaii is the only state to have been an independent **monarchy**.

When British explorers first arrived, Polynesians greeted them with open arms.

Early American settlers came to Hawaii because of the economic promise of the sugarcane industry. Most of this industry came under their power.

The development of military facilities in Hawaii brought many American soldiers and sailors to the islands in the 1930s.

The exact date of arrival of the first settlers to the Hawaiian Islands is unknown. Historians believe that it was sometime between the seventh and thirteenth centuries.

Until 1848, the king owned all the land in Hawaii. He granted or rented various areas to chiefs or to people from other countries. In 1848, a new system was introduced. It divided the land and allowed commoners and foreigners to buy territory. The possibility of private ownership of Hawaiian land encouraged foreigners to invest in the area.

Sugarcane is grown on 70,000 acres of Kauai and Maui, producing 340,000 tons of raw sugar.

Hawaii's sugar industry was already flourishing by the time foreigners were allowed to buy land. Sugarcane production took on huge economic importance once American investors could purchase Hawaiian territory. The size and number of plantations grew. Soon, there was a shortage of Hawaiian workers for the fields. Plantation owners began to bring in laborers from China, Japan, the Philippines, and other areas of the world. This contributed to the vast cultural diversity that makes up Hawaii's population today.

Hawaiians make leis for decoration. Many people wear leis around their necks, as hat bands, or wrapped around their heads.

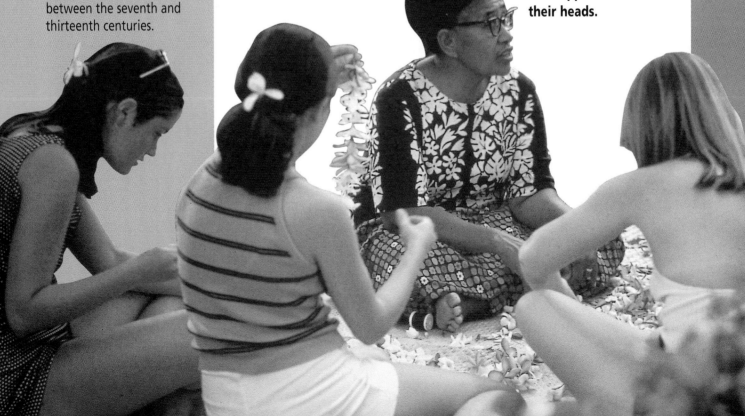

POPULATION

Hawaii is rich in ethnic and racial variety. People have come from all over the world to make their homes on the islands. Only about 12 percent of the people living in Hawaii today are descendants of the early Polynesians. The rest of Hawaii's population represents a variety of ethnic origins, including ties to Japan, China, the Philippines, Korea, Thailand, Vietnam, and Portugal.

Although Oahu is not the largest of the islands, 75 percent of the state's residents live there. The rest of the residents are spread out among the other islands. The Big Island has the second highest population, followed by Maui, Kauai, Molokai, and Lanai.

QUICK FACTS

About 1 million people live in Hawaii.

The male and female population is equal in Hawaii: Fifty percent of its inhabitants are men, and 50 percent are women.

Honolulu is the largest city in the state. The second largest is Hilo, on the island of Hawaii.

Hawaii is the most ethnically diverse state in the union.

Some Polynesian chants and songs were thought to be so special that the singers were very careful to pronounce every word properly.

POLITICS AND GOVERNMENT

The structure of Hawaii's local governments is different from any other state. There are no municipal governments in Hawaii. Instead, all local government functions are divided among four counties. The four counties of the state of Hawaii are the County of Hawaii; the County of Honolulu; the County of Kauai, which includes Kauai and Nihau; and the County of Maui, which includes Maui, Lanai, Kahoolawe, and nearly all of Molokai. A mayor and a council govern each county.

A fifth county in Hawaii, the county of Kalawao, consists of the northern part of Molokai. This area is a settlement for people with **leprosy**. Because leprosy is an infectious disease, the U.S. State Department of Health governs the County of Kalawao.

QUICK FACTS

Queen Liliuokala was the last reigning monarch of Hawaii. She was overthrown in 1893 by a group of American businessmen who were threatened by the power of the monarchy. An official transfer of Hawaiian power to the United States took place in 1898.

On June 14, 1900, Hawaii became an American territory. Hawaiian citizens became U.S. citizens.

The United States military began to build a large naval base at Pearl Harbor on the island of Oahu. On December 7, 1941, Japanese fighters attacked Pearl Harbor. The military lost lives, ships, and aircraft. The attack prompted America's entry into World War II.

The Constitution of Hawaii came into effect when it became a state in 1959.

Hawaii has twenty-five members in the Senate and fifty-one in the House of Representatives.

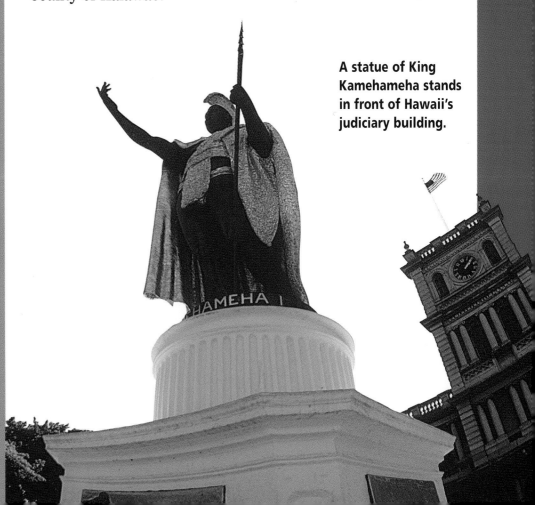

A statue of King Kamehameha stands in front of Hawaii's judiciary building.

CULTURAL GROUPS

Hawaiian society is a pleasant mix of cultures and customs. The various cultural groups living on the islands all contribute to the colorful life of the state. People in Hawaii celebrate their distinctive culture through their language, festivals, and food.

Hawaii has two official languages: Hawaiian and English. Almost everyone in Hawaii speaks English. The Hawaiian language, which is descended from the Polynesian settlers, is almost extinct. However, the language is still present in the names of places and in songs. People on the islands also use words from the Hawaiian language in their everyday speech. English mixed with Hawaiian is heard regularly. Other languages are also heard. Immigrants from China, Japan, and the Philippines often speak their native languages.

QUICK FACTS

There are only twelve letters in the Hawaiian alphabet: a, e, h, i, k, l, m, n, o, p, u, w.

Every August 21, Hawaii celebrates Admission Day, which is the anniversary of its statehood.

June 11 is Kamehameha Day. On this day, Hawaiians honor the man who united their islands.

Many Chinese people came to Hawaii in the late 1800s to work as field hands on sugar plantations.

One of Hawaii's most famous customs is the traditional lei greeting. A lei is a wreath of flowers strung together and worn as a necklace. Visitors to the islands are often presented with a lei as a sign of welcome. Hawaiian people wear leis during festivals and celebrations.

In Hawaii, it is customary to remove your shoes before entering someone's home. This tradition stems from Japanese culture.

Hawaii's many festivals and events celebrate its diverse culture. Hawaiians observe Chinese New Year, which falls in January or February. Japanese **bon dances** are performed in July or August to honor their dead ancestors. Festivals honoring Filipino culture are also celebrated. In the fall, the Aloha Festival celebrates Hawaiian culture with parades, races, dancing, and huge feasts.

Since the word for skirt in Hawaii is "Pa'u," women who rode horses were called "Pa'u Riders." Today, Pa'u Riders attend many festivals and parades.

The term hula refers to movements and gestures. However, hula cannot be performed without *mele*, or poetry.

ARTS AND ENTERTAINMENT

Hawaii has many foods that are unique to the state. You can find all of these foods at a traditional feast called a luau. The main feature of the luau is a whole roasted pig called a **kalua** pig. The pig is roasted in a huge pit called an imu. You will also find **poi** at a luau. Poi is a starchy paste made from the root of a taro plant. Traditionally, people do not eat poi with utensils. They scoop it out of a bowl with their fingers. Another type of food typically found at a luau is **laulau**. Laulau is pork, fish, or chicken wrapped with other ingredients in the leaves of the **ti** plant.

Hawaiians celebrate good times with a feast called a luau. They thank the gods for their good luck.

The Bishop Museum was named for Princess Bernice Pauahi Bishop, the last descendent of the royal Kamehameha family.

Bette Midler, a famous singer and actress, was born in Honolulu on Dec 1, 1945.

The island of Kauai was featured in Steven Spielberg's film *Jurassic Park*.

The Honolulu Symphony Orchestra was formed in 1902. The orchestra performs in Honolulu and on the other major islands.

Food is not the only feature of a **luau**. There is usually traditional dancing and music as well. Hula dancing is the most famous type of dancing on the islands. Hula dancers move their hips and arms gracefully. Their movements reveal a story or describe the beauty of the islands.

The dancers move to the music of the Hawaiian guitar and the **ukulele**, among other instruments. The ukulele was adapted from a small guitar brought to the islands by Portuguese workers in the late 1800s. The Hawaiian guitar, which was developed in Hawaii around 1895, is a steel guitar. Both instruments are an important part of Hawaiian music.

Hawaiians have a great appreciation for art and promote all forms of it in the state. The Honolulu Academy of the Arts has a large collection of western art. The Bishop Museum, also in Honolulu, is dedicated to the study and conservation of the history and culture of the Pacific and its people. The museum's displays include archeological discoveries, fish, shells, and plants from the Pacific Islands.

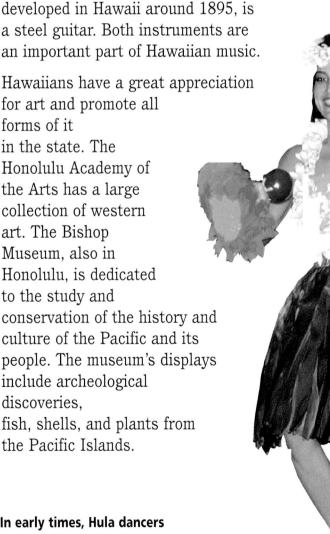

In early times, Hula dancers were dedicated to Laka, goddess of the Hula.

SPORTS

Hawaii is a tropical playground. Its mild climate encourages locals and tourists to take part in many outdoor sports and recreational events. Golf courses and tennis courts are regular features throughout the islands. Some of the most beautiful golf courses in the world are in Hawaii.

There are scenic bicycle paths and hiking trails on all the islands. Hikers and cyclists can explore the massive volcanoes, lush rain forests, and green valleys of Hawaii. Guided nature walks and **ecotours** are also popular. Hawaiian people are proud of their land and will happily share its beauty with anyone who wishes to honor it.

QUICK FACTS

Baseball is a favorite sport on the islands. The Hawaiian Baseball League teams are a symbol of pride for various ethnic communities.

The Molokai to Oahu canoe race takes place every October. The fastest recorded time is 4 hours and 53 minutes for the 40.8 mile course.

Swimming in Hawaii is especially pleasurable because there is little difference between water and air temperatures.

The Hawaiian Islands have biking trails that allow cyclists to view the many historic sites.

The islands are excellent for watersports. Scuba diving and snorkeling are very popular pastimes. Hawaii's underwater scenery is spectacular. Not only do divers get to swim among colorful fish, but they also get to see amazing natural architecture. During the formation of the islands millions of years ago, molten lava spilled into the sea and cooled to form incredible structures. Deep in the ocean, there are huge cave-like rooms, archways, and tunnels—all made from lava.

Surfing is a popular watersport in Hawaii. Surfers from all over the world come to Hawaii to ride the waves. Beginners can take surfing lessons on Waikiki Beach.

The steady wind and surf conditions in Hawaii have helped to make it one of the best windsurfing spots in the world. International windsurfing competitions are often hosted by Oahu.

QUICK FACTS

Duke Kahanamoku is one of Hawaii's most famous athletes. He won Olympic gold medals in the 1912 and 1920 Olympics for the 100-meter race in swimming. He was also the first person to be inducted into The Surfing Hall of Fame.

The Aloha Stadium hosts a variety of sports teams.

You can downhill ski on the upper portions of Mauna Loa and Mauna Kea. Snow covers their peaks during the winter months.

Marine life in Hawaii greatly differs from other tropical islands. These islands are quite isolated and were formed by volcanoes.

Brain Teasers

1

Checking Age

Which is the oldest of the Hawaiian Islands?

a. Hawaii

b. Kauai

c. Oahu

Answer: b. Kauai

2

What kind of musical instrument is called the leaping flea?

a. the accordion

b. the kazoo

c. the ukulele

Answer: c. the ukulele. Ukulele is a Hawaiian word meaning "leaping flea."

3

What famous American aviator is buried in Maui?

a. Charles Lindbergh

b. Amelia Earhart

c. Orville Wright

Answer: a. Charles Lindbergh

4

True or False

Hawaii's Mauna Kea volcano is taller than Mount Everest.

Answer: True. If you measure Mauna Kea from its base on the ocean floor to its peak, its height is 33,476 feet. Mount Everest is 29,108 feet.

5

True or False

There are no more Hawaiian islands developing.

Answer: False. Bubbling lava is slowly building another island, which is due to emerge in about 10,000 years.

7

TRUE OR FALSE?

The Kilauea eruption of 1983 has not yet ended.

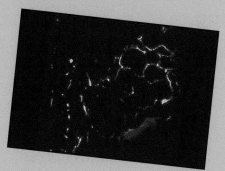

Answer: True. Lava is still flowing from the 1983 eruption.

6

TRUE OR FALSE

POGs are named after a popular Hawaiian beverage called passion-orange-guava drink.

Answer: True. The bottle tops were called POGs for short.

8

Here is a list of Hawaiian words. See if you can find a pattern in the arrangement of letters.

Hale (hah lay): house
Huhu (hoo hoo): angry
Kane (kah neh): man
Kaukau (kow kow): food
Moana (moh ah nah): ocean
Ohana (oh hah nah): family
Wahine (wah hee nay): woman

Did you notice anything special about the formation of these words?

Answer: Every word in the Hawaiian language ends in a vowel. Consonants never appear without a vowel between them.

FOR MORE INFORMATION

Books

Fradin, Dennis B., *Hawaii*. Children's Press, 1997.

Lovett, Sarah. *Kidding Around the Hawaiian Islands*. Santa Fe: 1990.

Nelson, Sharlene. *Hawaii Volcanoes National Park*. Toronto: HarperCollins Canada, 1998.

Thompson, Kathleen. *Hawaii*. Austin, TX: Raintree Steck-Vaughn, 1996.

Web sites

Find your Hawaiian name at http://www.hisurf.com/hawaiian/names.html

For up to date information and statistics on all aspects of Hawaiian history and culture, go to the government page: http://www.hawaii.gov

Find out about Hawaii's volcanoes at http://www.nps.gov/havo/

Go on a virtual field trip to the Hawaiian Islands at http://satftp.soest.hawaii.edu/space/hawaii/virtual.filed.trips.html

Visit Hawaii's home page at http://www.hawaii.net

Some web sites stay current longer than others. To find more Hawaii web sites, use your Internet search engines to look up such topics as "Hawaii," "Polynesia," "volcano," "luau," or any other topic you want to research.

GLOSSARY

barren: not producing, unfruitful

bon dances: Japanese Buddhist festival held every year to honor the dead

ecotours: tours to places that have unspoiled natural resources

eroding: slowly wearing away

immunities: ability to fight infections and diseases

import: to bring an item into a state or country from another part of the country or world

islets: small islands

kalua: Hawaiian word for the pig at a luau

laulau: meat wrapped in ti leaves, a Hawaiian dish

leprosy: a contagious disease

luau: a great Hawaiian feast

lush: full and plentiful with plant life

monarch: a king, queen, or someone who rules over a kingdom

patron: a person who gives financial or other kinds of help to another person

poi: a Hawaiian food made from the root of the taro plant

Polynesia: a group of islands in the Pacific Ocean

port: a harbor

taro: a tropical plant that can be eaten

ti: a tree or shrub found in Hawaii, with edible roots and leaves

trade wind: a steady wind

ukulele: a small guitar-like musical instrument

Union Jack: the national flag of Britain

INDEX